DRAWING on COURAGE

DRAWING on COURAGE

Risks Worth Taking and Stands Worth Making

Ashish Goel

Illustrations by Ruby Elliot

TEN SPEED PRESS
California | New York

HASSO PLATTNER
Institute of Design at Stanford

Contents

THANKSSSSS

A Note from the d.school

At the Stanford d.school, *design* is a verb. It's an attitude to embody and a way to work. The core of that work is trying, to the best of one's abilities, to help things run more smoothly, delight more people, and ease more suffering. This holds true for you, too—whether design is your profession or simply a mindset you bring to life.

Founded in 2005 as a home for wayward thinkers, the d.school was a place where independent-minded people could gather, try out ideas, and make change. A lot has shifted in the decade or so since, but that original exuberant and resourceful attitude is as present today as it was then.

Our series of guides is here to offer you the same inventiveness, insight, optimism, and perseverance that we champion at the d.school. Like a good tour guide, these handbooks will help you find your way through unknown territory and introduce you to some fundamental ideas that we hope will become cornerstones in your creative foundation.

Explore the critical skill of making decisions amid the unknown in *Navigating Ambiguity*. Decipher the mysteries and storytelling power of data in *The Secret Language of Maps*. And in this little book, learn to thwart all that stands in the way of doing work that matters.

Welcome to *Drawing on Courage*!

love,
the d.school

SHEEP IN WOLF'S CLOTHING

CHICKEN OUT CARDS

WHAT IS THIS?

AMERICAN EGGSPRESS
GET OUT FREE
COWARD CREDIT

UMM, IT MAGICALLY TELEPORTS ME OUT OF THE WOODS.

OSTRICH NECK PILLOW

WHOA!

WELL, IT KEEPS ME COMFY WHEN I CAN'T HIDE.

ELECTRONIC CONFORMIFIER

AND THIS?

EH... IT LETS ME AVOID TAKING A STAND IN CASE WE ENCOUNTER STRONG-WILLED WOODFOLK

AND THIS?

SENDS ME INTO A TIZZY SO I CAN MAKE A QUICK EXIT

HEEBIE JEEBIES

HEEBIE JEEBIES TRAIL MIX

SO YOU'RE AS SCARED AS I AM! WHY DON'T I HAVE ANY OF THIS?

I FIGURED IF PUSH COMES TO SHOVE, I'LL LET THEM GET YOU FIRST.

AWKWARD SILENCE

Introduction:
Why Courage?

You might look back at moments in your life and your work, as I do, and wish you had acted more courageously. You probably knew then what was the right thing to do (or at least you know now what you should have done), but you didn't do it. You chickened out.

This moment may have felt monumental or minor: leaving home to move to a new city, speaking up for a cause you believe in, asking someone out, having a difficult conversation, getting up on stage, trying something new, voicing an opinion that might have been unpopular among your peers, asking for help, and on and on.

Acting with courage is hard. You are taking a risk, and that's scary. Yet you have to act with courage—even though you may not be ready, the conditions aren't ideal, or you are venturing into unknown territory. Why? Because courage is the precursor to all change. Without courage, the status quo remains the status quo.

Design is also about challenging the status quo, be it the impossible curves in the buildings of a world-class architect like Zaha Hadid, the inventive installation art of a graphic designer like Stefan Sagmeister, or anything in between. It all takes courage.

But, this book isn't just about designing with courage. It is about *couraging* with *design*. Couraging with design means using the tools of design to be more courageous—no matter who you are or what you do. Just as designers sketch out ideas to see if they're any good, you can do the same with your fears to see if they're really as bad as they seem. Just as designers "prototype" to test concepts, you can try out things that feel a little risky. Just as designers craft catchy slogans to capture your attention, you can use language to shape your own actions.

My Story

I noticed my courage gap during a stint as the head of design at Zomato, one of the biggest technology startups in India.

I pride myself on being a quick learner. When I encounter something new or difficult, my reflex is to bridge the gaps in my knowledge with research, skills, and tools. When I'm struggling to convince my project's stakeholders, I seek to get better at negotiation and articulating the principles and values that inform the solution. If I'm not seeing eye to eye with my team, I might learn more about communication and coaching. When I'm working on a new project, perhaps I take a class.

Sure, additional knowledge, skills, and tools can be helpful, but they are not always enough.

> » As an employee, knowing the right design principles and negotiation skills didn't make it less scary to stand up for those principles and values.

THE OTHER SIDE

» As a manager, understanding the principles of good communication didn't make it less uncomfortable for me to have honest conversations, give and receive feedback, or let someone go.

» As a designer, learning new tools didn't make it less embarrassing to show my early work.

Once I noticed this pattern in my work, I could see it in other parts of my life too.

Without courage, the act of collecting skills and knowledge can become a kind of waiting: Waiting to get better. Waiting to get ready. Waiting for conditions to improve. Waiting for the path to reveal itself. Waiting for someone to give you permission. In sum: not acting.

You might be waiting to act, too. But if you wait for too long to leap to the other side, sometimes there is no other side left. The moment passes you by. Courage is making the leap when you must—not only when you're ready.

This book is about that leap, and about the journey you must take both before and after. Following are the four key stops along way.

1 The fear that blocks you.

2 The values that bolster you.

3 The moment of action.

4 The change that ensues.

Let's begin.

COURAGE...

THE ABILITY TO DO SOMETHING THAT FRIGHTENS ONE.

OXFORD DICTIONARY

CAPACITY TO RESIST A STRONG BUT UNJUST OPPONENT.

IMMANUEL KANT

GRACE UNDER PRESSURE.

ERNEST HEMINGWAY

MY 27TH STUDIO ALBUM.

CÉLINE DION

HOW VULNERABLE YOU ARE.

BRENÉ BROWN

REMOVING THE HEADPHONE JACK FROM THE IPHONE.

APPLE'S MARKETING CHIEF

1

What Is Courage?

Plato named courage (which he called "fortitude") as one of the four cardinal virtues. *The Oxford English Dictionary* defines it as "the ability to do something that frightens one." Ernest Hemingway, in a personal letter to the novelist F. Scott Fitzgerald, called it "grace under pressure." (To be precise, Hemingway didn't use the word *courage.* Dorothy Parker, who profiled Hemingway for the *New Yorker,* assumed he was referring to courage with that phrase.) When Apple launched an iPhone without a headphone jack, Apple's marketing chief described the choice as "the courage to do something new." How do we pin down the meaning of a word that is both a cardinal virtue and marketing speak?

So, what is courage? To answer this question, a group of researchers from four universities—Yale, Penn State, the U.S. Air Force Academy, and Tufts—had an idea. They crafted thirty-three short stories featuring protagonists who were faced with a decision entailing different levels of risk and reward. Then they asked regular people to read the stories and decide when the protagonists had shown courage.

The researchers found that nearly everyone polled considered the protagonists to be courageous when three factors were present:

> **The person was motivated by a worthy (often noble) purpose.** This could be saving someone, standing up to injustice, or just following through with a personal challenge.

THE COMPONENTS OF COURAGE

There was personal risk involved. They could have been hurt by their actions or lost their social standing.

Their actions were voluntary. They made a choice and took responsibility for it, no matter what.

The researchers made a second observation that is equally illuminating: courage is an "exceptional response to specific external conditions." It is not something you have or don't have. It is not a fixed trait. Courage is how you behave in a certain situation. All of us can act with courage when we need to.

So "What is courage?" is not even the right question. A far more useful inquiry is "When is courage?" What are the circumstances that make courage happen? And how can you create those circumstances in your own life?

Before I answer those questions, here's one more. Aren't there differences between courageous acts, regardless of when they happen? You may be thinking that the courage to begin working on a new idea or change careers is not the same courage that's required to leap into the waves to save a drowning child. We tend to associate courage with big, momentous acts. And momentous acts do require courage, but so do the small acts of courage that we face on a daily basis.

Epic and Everyday Courage

Shahnaz Bukhari, a civil rights activist, founded the Progressive Women's Association in Pakistan to help victims of domestic violence. She converted her own home into a shelter, uncovered thousands of cases of violence, and was even arrested on the false charge of "abetting an attempt to commit adultery." In 2003 she was awarded the Civil Courage Prize for her work, recognizing her "steadfast resistance to evil at great personal risk." Now *that*, you would say, is courage. And you would be correct.

I call this epic courage. (And may we all have epic courage when the time comes.)

But countless moments that don't result in awards still call for courage: Holding an unpopular opinion. Having a difficult conversation. Standing up for yourself. Standing up for someone else. Doing the right thing. Doing things right. Starting something new. Not quitting when it gets old. Beginning again. Trusting another person. Trusting yourself. Giving feedback. Getting feedback. Speaking up versus going with the herd. Doing what is ethical and not just economical.

This is everyday courage.

Epic and everyday courage are different in a few ways:

Epic courage—because it's, well, epic—draws attention and recognition (and sometimes apathy and scorn). **Everyday courage** is what you notice and feel personally, even if no one else does.

Epic courage is not only risky but also could be ruinous. **Everyday courage** is risky for sure, but also easier to recover from.

Epic courage seems like one momentous event; **everyday courage** is lots of little actions.

But here's the thing: everyday courage can have epic results. Big, systemic changes build bit by bit over time. Whether the system is your family, your workplace, a school, or a country, within that system your everyday choices and everyday courage (or lack of it) add up—for better or worse. Moreover, these little acts can prepare you to rise to an epic moment if need be. Everyday courage is the fuel for your ingenuity and the midwife of your integrity.

Alright. We know what courage looks like (you take a risk, follow a purpose, and choose to act), and we have a context for when to practice it (every day), but what does it mean to actually be courageous?

The Journey of Courage

You rarely think about the idea of courage in the midst of a difficult situation or dilemma. Instead you act (or fail to act) based on how you feel:

> **You feel scared about the risks ahead.**

> **Your gut tells you that you must do something— it is the right thing to do.**

> **You wonder:** *Should I be the one doing this? Am I being bold, or merely stupid?*

It is this moment-by-moment *journey* that you must navigate when you are faced with circumstances that call for courage.

Every courageous journey has several stops along the way. Like levels in an existential video game, they are filled with traps to avoid, demons to thwart, and rewards to gather.

Stop 1: Fear

Fear comes first. It appears when you start to see potential risks on the horizon. You begin to feel uncertain about how things will play out, see looming unpleasant consequences, and wonder if you will be able to rise to the challenges ahead. Fear is a constant companion on your journey.

THE COURAGE JOURNEY

FEARSOME FOREST

NO, DON'T!

FEATURING FEAR, A FORMIDABLE FOE THAT TAKES ANY FORM TO COMBAT YOUR COURAGE.

VALUES BRIDGE

FEATURING VALUES AND PURPOSE, YOUR PARTNERS IN THWARTING FEAR'S NASTY ANTICS.

YOU WANT TO MAKE A DIFFERENCE.

AND THAT'S WHY THIS RISK IS WORTH TAKING.

Stop 2: Values

Your values form a scaffold to support you on your journey. Values motivate and make risk-taking worthwhile. When I say *values,* I'm using the word broadly. It can refer to a personal goal or the action of upholding your morals or ethics. Your values can also be causes or purposes that drive you. You might not always be able to give voice to your values, but they're there, guiding you forward.

Stop 3: Action

Making a choice and acting of your own volition is the "when" of courage. Action is your response to a dilemma or situation in the face of fear. Often, we get right to the point of action—and retreat. We chicken out.

Stop 4: Change

What happened as a result of your actions—what changed? Even when nothing else changes, *you* change. This is the moment when you must adapt, reorient, and respond to new circumstances.

These are the stops on any courage journey. By zooming out on your particular journey, you can see where you are, figure out why you are stuck, and then decide what to do.

In the following chapters, we will visit each of these stops to learn what they feel like and how you can navigate them.

Fear is our first stop. Here we go . . .

WHO'S THERE?

2

Fear

We all have fears. They range from the tiny and mundane to the big and hairy.

Michael Bernard Loggins, an artist and list maker, wrote down 138 such fears in his zine *Fears of Your Life*. They ranged from common ones, like fear of going to the doctor and fear of authority and punishment, to offbeat gems, like fear of dropping a soda and having it fizz all over.

At the heart of each of these fears is risk: the possibility that something may go wrong. And most of the time, things don't really go wrong. But when you take a risk to do something that matters to you, your fears amp up. For instance, you might be scared:

> **To speak up because you might face ridicule or hostility.**

> **To start something new because you could fail.**

> **To have a difficult conversation because it could lead to conflict or, worse, a falling-out with a colleague or loved one.**

> **To admit a mistake, because that can make you seem foolish.**

Neuroscientist and behavioral scientist Antonio Damasio was among the first to show the role that emotions play in decision-making. One of his patients, code-named Elliot, suffered damage to his frontal lobe that impaired his ability to feel and experience emotion. Although Elliot could reason and make logical statements, the damage made it impossible for him to make decisions.

In short, feelings affect actions. And fear is a big feeling. You encounter it as soon as you start your courage journey, and it stops you from moving forward.

One scenario where fear almost always shows itself is when you start doing work that is personally meaningful to you but does not come with any assurance of success or rewards. It's self-directed work that no one is asking you to do: A cause you support. The art you make after hours. Or something bigger, like writing a novel or running for local office.

As you start this work, you wonder: *Should I even try? I have no clue how or where to begin.* This is the fear of the unknown. If you manage to drown out those doubts, and even make some progress, then the fear of incompetence shows up, whispering: *What if the thing I create isn't as good as what I imagined?* And before you can even address it, the fear of inconsequence chimes in, asking: *Hasn't this been done before?* And that is when the fear of missing out throws on the last straw by announcing: *Leave this. I've got a bunch of other exciting ideas to work on.*

Steven Pressfield, a successful writer who wrote for twenty-seven years before his first novel got published, refers to the force that stops us from doing what we must as "resistance." He writes in his book *The War of Art,* "It will assume any form, if that's what it takes to shove us away, distract us, prevent us from doing our work."

Fear is a shapeshifter. It assumes the avatar that is most effective for its purposes, which is to stop you from doing this work.

FEAR THE SHAPESHIFTER

ENOUGH'S ENOUGH.

THAT PROJECT I'VE BEEN STEWING ON FOREVER? I'M GOING TO DO IT.

UH-OH

SHAPE?

SHIFT

FEAR OF THE UNKNOWN

BIG SOUPY PROJECTS

AHEM, WE DEFINITELY DON'T KNOW HOW TO DO THIS, BETTER TO QUIT NOW. WE KNOW QUITTING. LOVELY, SAFE QUITTING.

Each of these moments might feel different from the rest, but they are all just examples of fear shifting shape and trying out different ways to thwart you. That's not to say that you have nothing to be afraid of. Though fear is a shapeshifter, it is not always wrong. You might fail. That's real. Failure has consequences, and fear sometimes helps point them out. Still, it can be hard to tell when your fear is on point or off-kilter.

Courage and fear are dance partners. You can't have one without the other. The ever-quotable Mark Twain wrote, "Courage is resistance to fear, mastery of fear—not the absence of fear." So the fears will not go away, and that is okay. The problem is when fears prevent you from starting the work that matters to you in the first place, or abandoning it too early.

Soon those unfinished projects turn into an endless backlog. It's an all-you-can-eat buffet gone horribly wrong. Not only is your plate spilling over with your own selections, but it also contains the side project sushi your friend said you must try, a bigger helping of writing resolution risotto than you needed, the volunteering veal you thought you'd like but didn't, and . . . how on earth did those sliders get in there?

Whether your fear is stopping you from doing meaningful work, standing up for what's right, or something else, you must:

Unmask your fear to expose its machinations.

Get used to it.

When possible, remove it altogether.

Fear: Unmask It

The first thing you can do is to recognize these internal warnings for what they are: manifestations of your fear. Then you can decide which ones are valid and which ones are misplaced.

Writer and programmer Paul Ford suffered from anxiety, so he created a spambot to help him deal with it. As he tells it on the podcast *Reply All,* he entered his anxieties into a program that turned them into emails and sent them back to him several times a day. Stuff like, "Hi Paul, history will forget you, because history forgets people who are unable to finish things." (He was trying to finish a novel.) Or personal insults like "People look at your internet profile and think: in possession of a weird nose."

Sounds a bit nuts, right? Wouldn't this make his anxiety worse? It didn't. Instead, it helped to make his fears look like junk mail, the kind you can ignore or quickly delete. It kept his fears from playing in a loop in his head. Sometimes the best way to get over a fear is to acknowledge it.

Patricia Ryan Madson, a Stanford drama faculty member and the founder of Stanford Improvisers, has taught hundreds of students to get over their stage fright. She puts it like this in her book, *Improv Wisdom:* "Fear is not the problem; allowing your attention to be consumed by it is."

So check in with your fears. What do they sound like? What do they look like? Are they jagged or smooth? Sarcastic or sassy? Ruthless or cold? Once you identify your fears, you're one step closer to tapping the courage you need in order to face them—and defeat them.

FEAR'S SPEAKEASY

Shrink Your Fear

Designers often make sketches, prototypes, or simple lists when they start working on any problem. They don't do it only once they know the answer, but as a way to *get* to the answer. Nigel Cross, a researcher who has studied how designers work, noted in his book *Design Thinking* that "Designing is difficult to conduct by purely internal mental processes. An external representation provides a temporary, external store for tentative ideas, and supports the 'dialogue' that the designer has between problem and solution."

Once you externalize an idea, you can respond to it. Apply this same tactic to your fears. Pick something you have been avoiding out of fear. List or sketch what scares you about it. Your descriptions will often start with phrases like "I'm afraid of . . . " or "I worry that . . . " or "I am anxious about . . . " And they are likely to fall into one of four buckets:

> **Currently irrelevant:** I worry that I'm too old to start a novel. (What does age have to do with writing a novel?)
>
> **Completely baseless:** I am afraid I won't stand up for myself because I cannot deal with conflict. (Yes, you avoided conflict that one time, but no, that does not make you a serial chicken-outer.)
>
> **Mildly mortifying:** I'm afraid people won't like my speech. (Sure, there will be a few people who might dislike your talk, but isn't that always the case?)
>
> **Legitimately scary:** If I leave this job, start a company, and fail, I may blow up my savings. (True enough; *that's* a real risk.)

continued »

FEAR DRAWN TO SCALE

Shrink Your Fear, continued

In Stoicism, a school of philosophy, this practice is called negative visualization. It's a process of mentally playing out the worst-case scenario, imagining what could happen if you do what you are scared of. Often, just making the list can stop your fears from consuming your attention.

Or, when needed, you can respond to your fears one by one. The currently irrelevant ones have nothing to do with the project you are embarking on; they might count, but not right now. The completely baseless are single incidents blown out of whack; you don't have to believe them. The mildly mortifying set you have to accept as part of your journey (we'll talk about getting used to your fears in a second), and the legitimately scary are those you have to guard against (we'll talk about reducing risk later on, too).

Fear: Get Used to It

While unmasking fear weakens it, this process alone doesn't make the fear go away. You need something more: you have to learn how to get accustomed to it.

Once you become used to how fear feels, you can take action in spite of it. Psychologists use *exposure therapy* to help their patients get accustomed to their fears. To help a patient overcome a fear of needles, for instance, a therapist might start by simply showing the patient the needle. In subsequent sessions, the therapist moves the needle progressively closer, until the patient gets so used to seeing it and having it nearby that they no longer feel afraid.

Jason Comely, a Canadian entrepreneur, created his own game in the vein of exposure therapy to take the sting out of being told no. He dubbed it "Rejection Therapy." Handling rejection well is a useful skill for anyone who works in sales, runs a business, auditions, or submits creative work. I learned it from a friend who tried it for a behavior design class at Stanford. The one rule of this exercise is that you must get rejected at least once a day. He tried making requests that were unlikely to be granted. "Can I get an extension on that assignment?" "May I come in, even though you're closing in five minutes?" Of course, the answers were not always no. You don't know what you can get unless you ask. But he asked enough people to hear at least one no every day. By the way, this is not a suggestion to engage in selfish behavior. His goal was to get used to hearing no so he wouldn't be scared of hearing it.

This approach of taking small risks to experience the feeling of fear is useful in other contexts, too. How can you get used to your fears when it comes to doing work that matters? Risk creating something you feel is not good enough. Treat it as raw material. Really! Then you have something to work with—even if that *something* isn't so great. Author Shannon Hale hints at it when she describes the intent behind her very first drafts: "I have to remind myself constantly that I'm only shoveling sand into a box so later I can build sandcastles."

You might feel that generating crummy work is wasteful. Michael Dearing, an investor who has also taught at the d.school and has shepherded many entrepreneurs through the early days of their ventures, suggests you think of this work as "not waste, but compost." Your efforts are not wasted because you can use the material to improve and build something new.

The first pancake always ends up in the trash. The lesson applies whether you're talking about breakfast or passion projects. Being willing to create bad work first in order to create good work later on is not just an act of courage (taking a risk for something that matters); it really is the only way to create at all, and the only way to get used to fear in all of its shapeshifting avatars.

IT'S COMPOST, NOT WASTE

A Risky Streak

Taking one small risk will not help you get used to your fears. What you need is a streak. A Risky Streak involves taking a tiny risk every day for a certain number of days as a way to strip your fear of its power.

Scared to ask a question in a class? Raise your hand once each day.

Uncomfortable in social settings? Say hello to a stranger each day.

Scared of getting started? Risk creating bad work (compost).

Scared of exposing your work to the world? Share a little bit of your work in whatever way makes sense.

Start by asking yourself: What am I afraid of that I would like to overcome? Think of a tiny or analogous risky behavior that you can do every day to experience that fear. Remember that fear is a shapeshifter. Don't get too hung up on what the *right* tiny risk is; just choose something that makes you feel a bit nervous.

How long should your streak last? Decide the duration and frequency up front (once-a-day-for-100-days, based on The 100 Day Project conceptualized by the designer Michael Bierut, is a good format).

HOP, SPLASH, DIVE, LEAP

Fear: Get Rid of It (When You Can)

Another way to wrestle your fears into submission is to lower the risks that drive them in the first place by having a safety net, a dare pack, a plan B (or C). Many entrepreneurs hold down day jobs while getting their dream businesses off the ground. Phil Knight, the founder of Nike, earned his CPA certificate and became an accountant while running his company. As he writes in his memoir, *Shoe Dog,* it gave him "something safe to fall back on when everything went bust," and it reduced his personal risk.

If what you are doing involves speaking truth to power, for instance, you may be able to reduce your personal risk by recruiting others and building coalitions. In 2016, the city of Bangalore was planning to build a large steel overpass (called a "flyover" in India) at a cost of around $250 million. The flyover would cut travel time to the airport by seven minutes, but in the process destroy more than 850 trees. Naresh Narasimhan, an architect and environmentalist, felt that this was not a worthy trade-off. So he posted a video of himself advocating for the environment, and he ended up kickstarting a citizen movement that killed the flyover project.

As he described it in a talk at the conference DesignUp, "When you are going up against big systems, if you go alone, you will be crushed." Narasimhan may not have not gotten far by himself, but as part of a movement, he felt empowered to take a collective risk that made a difference.

THE DARE PACK

One everyday context in which you can remove risks to reduce fear is collaborative work. Your work will often involve working with others, which comes with its own set of fears and frustrations. Red Burns, founder of the famed Interactive Telecommunications Program at New York University, described collaboration as wearing "the ill-fitting clothes of someone else's world" and dining on "the strange food of someone else's thought."

As you now know, fear shapeshifts whether you're working solo, with a partner, or in a group. On a team, you may fear being disliked. Your fear of embarrassment might prevent you from taking a risk or proposing an idea that's outside the ordinary. Or worse, your fear of becoming an outsider might make you conform to a popular opinion that goes against your personal values. When you let these fears shape your behavior, collaboration dies, and courage along with it.

What makes teams click? Google did a two-year study to answer this very question by observing internal teams across the organization. They found that teams thrive when the members feel a sense of *psychological safety*, a term coined by Harvard professor Amy Edmondson. This means that the team members had created a collaborative relationship in which there was no risk of being shamed or shunned for voicing conflicting opinions or being vulnerable in front of each other. To collaborate well you to have address the fears in doing collaborative work.

Getting to a place of psychological safety in any team takes time as you work together and learn to understand each other. Is there a way to get there faster? There is— and it relies on norms.

Norms are shared but unspoken rules about how people should behave in a group. They shape which ideas are welcome, who speaks, and the texture of how people work together. If you can make these norms visible or create new ones—especially ones that signal that it is okay to take a risk—you can create a space of psychological safety more quickly. How do you make norms visible? First, use new language. Second, try some tangible indicators that signal it's okay to take a risk.

In India, real or perceived hierarchy plays a role in how teams interact. Members might be too eager to accept ideas when they come from a superior. To counter this, Deepinder Goyal, the CEO of Zomato, a tech company I used to work for, would often say at the beginning of a discussion, "Listen, it is okay for us to spar." It was a simple reminder that the team could disagree with him, even though he was the CEO.

Tangible artifacts can be equally powerful. Bréne Brown, the well-known author and researcher who studies vulnerability, writes in her book *Dare to Lead* that her teammates write a phrase on a sticky note at the start of a meeting to give themselves permission to say what they might otherwise be afraid to say. The phrase might be as prosaic as "I give myself permission to ask for breaks if we need them," or something brave, such as "I give myself permission to speak up even though I am the only one here who isn't an expert."

By consciously stepping back to notice and then subvert the norms usually at play, and by creating your own agreed-upon rules, you can build a low-fear, high-courage environment.

Let's Get Physical

Here's an activity, based on psychologist Edward de Bono's book *Six Thinking Hats* (we use four here), to safely try new behaviors in a team.

We all default to a certain way of looking at a topic in a group setting. Yours could be a tendency to find gaps in an idea or to seek more information. By trying different modes, you can uncover your team's norms and identify your own defaults.

Create four cards, each with a color, a directive, and the beginning of a statement. For example:

> **Red:** Lead with emotions. Start statements with, "How I feel about this situation is . . . "

> **Green:** Generate new ideas and directions. Start statements with, "Ooh, what if we try . . . "

> **White:** Focus on facts and what is unquestionably true. Start statements with, "Here is what we know for sure . . . "

> **Black:** Be careful and cautious. Start statements with, "The challenge I see here is . . . "

Before you begin a team discussion, pull a card and ask all members of the group to adopt the stated stance (for example, if you pull out the red card, all team members should share their feelings about the situation). Reflect on how the conversation played out. What is a mode that some people were afraid to try? Why were they afraid? What unsaid norms cause those fears? How can you change those norms?

Fear: Conclusion

Whether it's starting a project that matters to you, speaking your mind in a team setting, or moving to a new city, you may avoid (or put off) doing these things out of fear. You might claim that you need more preparation, but often the truth is that you are scared.

Fear is a shapeshifter. Sometimes speaking with the voice of your inner critic, other times as a well-meaning avatar who's just being pragmatic, fear attempts to stop you either because the outcome is risky or out of a sense of self-protection. That can be good, but not always.

Fear is the first stop on your courage journey because it wants to stop you right at the beginning. And it won't go away—fear is along for the ride, and courage is when you act not without fear, but in spite of it. You can recognize fear's shapeshifting nature and thwart it, but you also need something equally powerful to push you past fear. Something that makes acting in spite of the risks ahead worth it.

That's the second stop of the fear journey: a purpose that drives you and the values you hold dear.

LOOK AT YOU TURNING RED!

VALUES, PURPOSE, AND FRIENDS

3

Values

If fear is the force that deters acts of courage, your values are what drives those acts to begin with.

For years, Neha Singh sent a monthly text to a group of women in Mumbai. The goal? To determine a location in the city where they could loiter—that is, hang out aimlessly—from midnight until 3 a.m. Women are rarely out late on the streets in India, even in supposedly woman-friendly Mumbai. It is unsafe, socially frowned on, and, in some cases, illegal.

Singh and her comrades loitered, and risked their physical safety, as a radical protest. Singh was inspired by Shilpa Phadke, a sociologist who writes in her book, *Why Loiter?,* that loitering is a feminist act, one that expands the definition of public space for women to have the right to work and also the right to have fun—or, as Phadke puts it, the "right to unadulterated, unsanctioned pleasure." Neha Singh was driven to act—in spite of fears and risks—because she valued this cause. It mattered to her.

What matters to you might be external—like a vision that inspires you or a cause that is meaningful to you, aka your *purpose.* Or it might be internal—a desire to stay true to your convictions, stand up for your beliefs, or simply do the right thing, aka your *values.*

It's not always easy to act for your purpose and from your values, but if an act seems to push you in a direction that supports your values, that act is often in the opposite direction of where your fear wants you to go.

Surfing the Wave of Fear

How can a clear and motivating set of values and purpose help you fight fear? Peruse the graph-slash-comic on page 42. As the perceived risks in a situation increase, so does your sense of fear. So when we plot fear against risk, we get a graph that looks like a wave. The low-risk area is the trough, the medium-risk area is the face, and the high-risk area is the crest. To act with courage you have to surf this wave. When you don't have a purpose that motivates you, no matter how risky (or safe) the action may be, you won't do it. You either don't care enough to wade into the waters at all, or if you find yourself in a tricky situation, you will choose to chicken out.

But when the purpose does motivate you, and you know you are standing up for things you truly value, you suddenly have a surfboard. Now you can ride that wave of fear.

The map shows, again, how everyday courage and epic courage are different. Everyday courage is the face of the wave, where things are risky but surfable. Epic courage lies at the crest of the wave, where it is high risk and high purpose with the occasional danger of martyrdom (gulp).

To ride the wave of fear, first you have to know what truly matters to you. In both your personal life and your role as a citizen in the world, clarifying and committing to your values and knowing what is worth standing up for give you courage when you need it.

SURF THE WAVE OF FEAR

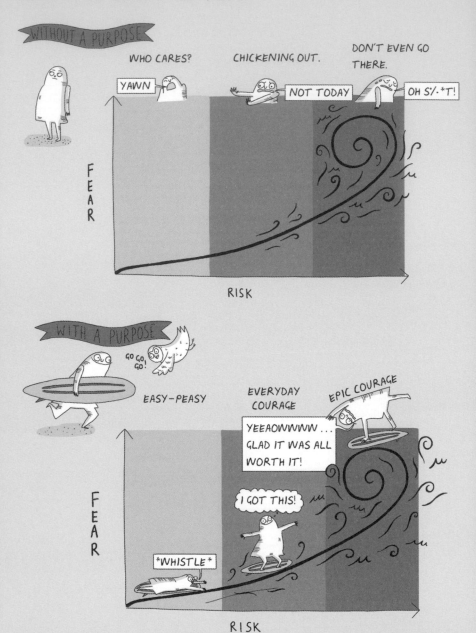

Find Your Purpose
and Values

One reason we don't choose to ride the wave of fear is that our purpose or values have become fuzzy or unclear.

Stanford psychologist William Damon describes purpose in his book *The Path to Purpose* as something "meaningful to the self *and* consequential for the world." Finding your purpose can take a whole lot of stumbling around before you figure it out. The same is true for your values, but they can be more amorphous. You may believe in personal values like authenticity and generosity, or ethical values like honesty and fairness. While you may consciously choose some values through experience, many come subconsciously through your culture, family, and community.

Fear loves this vagueness. What's more, your values may be idealistic or even naïve, and the risks of taking action are right in front of you. Robert Prentice, a professor at McCombs School of Business, studies behavioral ethics. In his 2014 article titled "Teaching Behavioral Ethics" in the *Journal of Legal Studies Education,* he observed that even when people are aware of their values, they may not act because they are "overwhelmed by social pressures, organizational stresses, and other situational factors."

Building a reflective practice to periodically examine your choices can help bring fuzzy values into focus and create a path forward. Reflection can be useful at three key moments of action: retrospectives, impasses, and inklings.

PURPOSE VENN-DING!

Retrospectives

Look back at a moment, choice, or project after you've taken action. Do you feel regret—wishing you had done things differently—or do you feel pride because the actions you took were in alignment with your values?

Impasses

When you hit a wall with your work, whether you have lost enthusiasm, feel disillusioned with your team or project, or are endlessly procrastinating over a decision—or when your fear rears its head—it's time to review your original intentions.

Inklings

You're moving forward with a clear rationale, but then suddenly you have a hunch, or a strong inkling, that's counter to your actions. This is another good time to stop and reflect.

Let these situations trigger you to step back and ask your-self some tough questions:

Why doesn't (or didn't) this decision sit well with me?

Why does this matter?

Am I staying true to my values?

A reflective practice will allow you to clarify and distill your purpose and values so that you can course-correct for the future or surf through a tough situation with courage.

LOOK BACK THROUGH THE ZOOM-OUT-O-SCOPE

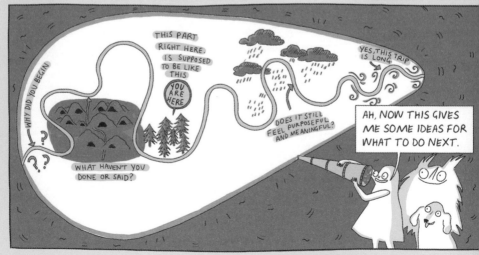

Origin Story

Here's one way to break an impasse in a personal project. It's easy to get caught up in the minutiae of your work and lose sight of why it matters. Reflecting on the beginnings of a project can help you recall the purpose behind it. By retracing your steps and renewing your commitment, you can keep going when the going gets tough. And it always gets tough. Remembering why you started, then writing it down, might give you the courage you need to keep showing up, especially when the results aren't quite what you expected or wanted (yet).

To flesh out the origin story of your work, ask yourself:

What was the sequence of events that led me to start working on this idea? Be as specific and detailed as possible. If you were stewing on it for a long time before you got cooking, what made you begin? If the decision to start was sudden, what triggered it?

What value was I trying to create or uphold for myself? Think broadly about values. They could be monetary, educational, cause-driven, and so on.

What value was I hoping to create for others?

Do I still resonate with my original intention or purpose?

What do I gain if I quit?

What do I lose if I keep going?

Stand Up for What You Believe

Finding the courage to stand up for what you value is especially consequential in the organizations and communities you belong to. When you are considering going against a given worldview, a popular or accepted norm, or the majority opinion, your actions are often thwarted by the fear of becoming an outsider. For instance:

A student trying to get the dorms to adopt recycling

A scientist whose idea runs counter to the prevailing theories

A recruiter who cares about diversity, working in a company that doesn't hire for diversity

A resident who cares about pedestrian walkways in their neighborhood

Donella Meadows, one of the foremost systems thinkers in the world, observed in her book *Thinking in Systems:* "Organizations and institutions are social systems, and they are shaped by shared value systems, assumptions, beliefs, ideologies, and worldviews, even if they are not always explicit." This is where everyday courage goes beyond the personal to the public—and can even have epic consequences. By standing up and showing up for what you value, even in small ways, you can make a difference.

It might not feel like you alone can effect big changes within huge systems, but our everyday acts shape the

SEAT AT THE TABLE

NOW?

TIM, WHAT DO YOU THINK?

I SPOKE UP ONCE, AND THEY MOVED ME OFF THE PROJECT. SO IT'S PROBABLY NOT WORTH IT...

A FAIR FEW PROJECTS LATER...

SEE?!

HEY! DON'T FORGET THESE!

STUFF I CARE ABOUT
- SUSTAINABILITY
- CRAFTSMANSHIP
- SAFETY COMPLIANCE

FINALLY, A PROMOTION!

WHUH? OH YEAH...

XYZ
XYZ

WAFFLE
WAFFLE

NOW'S YOUR CHANCE!

SHH I JUST GOT HERE, LET'S NOT ROCK THE BOAT.

BIG IDEA

PROPOSAL

world around us. Wilson Miner, a designer who created some of the earliest music streaming products, observed at the design conference Build that in moments of frustration he would often think, *It is just a website; it is not going to change the world. Let's get over it.* As someone who has worked in the world of software and websites for more than a decade, I admit that I have sometimes thought this too. And then he would remember the car. The car led to highways, factories, and oil companies. It changed our way of living. He mused that screens and algorithms, his media of work, may play a similar role in the twenty-first century, and they are. In the same way, you might feel that you are just a small component of a big community, organization, or system. Still, you do have a hand in shaping the world around you.

When it comes to acting with courage within an established system, we often refrain because fear enlists its good friends reason and comfort. When I asked Sneha Virmani, a product designer at a technology company, about this topic, she told me that it took courage for her to put the interests of customers ahead of meeting deadlines, pleasing managers, and prioritizing profits—aka going with the flow. Going with the flow is not necessarily the cowardly thing to do, but it is often the easier thing to do.

Can you go with the flow *and* change the status quo? Yes, you can. That's what everyday courage means. To facilitate change, you don't necessarily have to stand up in big ways without fail. Instead, you can stand up in small ways over and over again. How do you do it? I call it the Invitation Model.

The Invitation Model is a method for approaching change within a group, organization, or established system through many small acts. It has three parts.

Seek, by asking. Find out about the status quo. Become a sponge and learn why things are done as they are and what values already shape decisions and behaviors.

Show, by doing. Make what you value tangible. Create evidence, show results, and turn abstract values into concrete artifacts and outcomes.

Speak, by advocating. Craft stories that make people understand and care about what you're trying to do.

I was inspired to create the Invitation Model based on a conversation I had with Dave Evans, a beloved Stanford teacher, who also spent years working for companies like Electronic Arts and Apple. He said there are two ways to think about joining a new organization. One is "initiation": you go in with guns blazing, wanting to change everything. Or you can choose "invitation." You have been invited into an existing ecosystem; you need to first honor that ecosystem, understand it, and then find moments to bring change.

I love this framing. The Invitation Model is about accepting that change takes time. Groups that have been around for a while have a way of doing things, and any change is an outcome of many, many acts of everyday courage.

THE INVITATION MODEL

OOH, HELLO

WOW, NICE PAPER

YOU'RE INVITED

WHEE! I'M EXPERIMENTING

SPEAK: TELL STORIES TO MAKE OTHERS CARE

THIS IS HOW I MADE MY FLASK OF DREAMS.

SEEK: UNDERSTANDING AND BUILD TRUST

TELL ME A BIT MORE ABOUT HOW THINGS WORK HERE.

SURE!

SHOW: MAKE YOUR IDEAS AND VALUES VISIBLE AND TANGIBLE

Seek: Ask and Build Trust

Instead of beginning with your answer—how you think things should be done—seek first. Try to look beneath the surface. Start with the question: Why is this the way things are done?

Seek out stories to discover how things came to be before you arrived. Try to detect the mental models or ways in which your partners approach problems and make decisions. Observe how people engage with each other.

Seek widely and often. Ask questions about past decisions and policy that no one asks about any more. How did this policy come to be? Why is the lobby set up the way it is? How do decisions get made? When you seek first, you can operate from a place of understanding, align your ideas with the group's values, and build trust and bridges with other people.

Jim Ryan, dean of Harvard's Graduate School of Education, has a great way of capturing this mindset. He calls it one of his essential questions: "Wait, what?" In his book of the same name, he says, "Clarification is the first step toward understanding something—whether it is an idea, an opinion, a belief, or a business proposal." The "wait" in "Wait, what?" isn't optional. Ryan says it is a reminder to slow down and make sure you understand.

HOW TO SEA

GET YOUR FEET WET

PEEK UNDER THE SURFACE

EXPAND YOUR FIELD OF VISION

DO A DEEP DIVE

GLUP GLUP GURGLE

GURGLE GURGLE?

GLUP! GURGLE

LEARN FROM THE LOCALS

Show: Make the Invisible Visible

In the previous chapter, I talked about how unsaid or unarticulated norms in a team can be made visible using new vocabulary or physical objects (see page 34). This idea of making the invisible visible is fundamental to design work. When you make tangible your ideas and values, people around you will better understand your goals and perhaps even be inspired by them.

This process can take many forms. You could:

Run a simple experiment or prototype.

Create tools that can make the idea shareable and usable by other people.

Curate case studies of how other communities are applying this change.

Take accessibility, for example. Typically, designing for accessibility involves creating physical and digital environments to be usable by people with disabilities. However, in many companies this can often be an afterthought, and there are still many products and services that are not accessible. In her book *Mismatch,* tech design executive Kat Holmes discusses how she and her Microsoft team wanted to change this, so they broadened the concept of accessibility and expanded its value. They called it inclusive design.

By demonstrating that a device designed for a person with one hand was also useful to someone with situational limitations, such as a person with a wrist injury or a new parent holding an infant, they showed that a

TRY ON A DESIGNER HAT

SO HOW DO I INTRODUCE THINGS-I-CARE-ABOUT TO MY COLLEAGUES?

HMM... I HAVE AN IDEA!

THERE'S "THIS SMART AFFAIR"

BRIMMING WITH STORIES OF HOW OTHER COMMUNITIES ARE APPLYING IT.

OR PERHAPS THE "EXPERIMENTER'S CAP."

TO ADD AN ADVENTUROUS FLAVOR OF EXPEDITION.

"LE BERET COMME CA*" IS VERY POPULAR:

TEMPLATES AND TOOLS THAT OTHERS CAN APPLY.

(*FRENCH FOR "DO IT LIKE THAT")

THERE'S OUR "LET'S-DIG-IN" CAP.

TOGGLES WILL HELP IT STAY ON WHILE YOU (AND YOUR GROUP) GET YOUR HANDS DIRTY.

AND OF COURSE, THE "WE'RE IN IT TOGETHER" BIKE HELMET! SHAREHOLDER VALUE JUST BOUGHT ONE EARLIER TODAY AND IS LOOKING FOR A BUDDY FOR HER TANDEM BIKE RIDE!

LET'S TAKE 'EM ALL!

WHADDYA RECKON?

feature designed for disability is actually useful to everyone. According to their numbers, only twenty-six thousand people in the United States have lost the use of an upper extremity. But when they included users with situational impairments, the number of people they could potentially serve went up to twenty million.

Instead of operating from a place of moral superiority or a sense of righteousness—good motivations that can also make for ineffective arguments—Holmes was able to facilitate change by showing that doing good was actually good for business.

In their book *Tragic Design,* designers Jonathan Shariat and Cynthia Savard Saucier discuss their desire to reduce the use of dark user experience patterns in apps and websites. Dark user experience patterns exploit human psychology to dupe you, mislead you, and make you feel guilty—think about any time you've tried to close an account but instead landed in a ten-minute survey or an arm-twisting interview.

To counter these tactics, Shariat and Saucier invented antigoals: something a feature *should not* do. For the preceding example, the antigoals might be (1) don't add unnecessary friction by adding too many steps, and (2) don't use tactics that evoke emotions like guilt or shame. They made their intention tangible.

What is something that you care about in your community? Make it more tangible or visible to show your peers how it can be applied.

Double Delivery

Double delivery is when you create two variants of a project. One version is what was expected (the go-with-the-flow version), and the other is the one you think can make a difference (the challenge-the-status-quo version).

This idea comes from IDEO. As Suzanne Gibbs Howard, a partner at the firm, explains on the *IDEO U* blog, she and her colleagues have often used this approach to embody a value they really care about: empathy. Many of IDEO's clients prefer to work with hard numbers and quantitative data. So Howard's team often double delivers and shows how qualitative learnings from a frame of empathy can make a difference.

DO IT LIKE THIS. DO IT LIKE THAT.

Speak: Shape the Zeitgeist

Speaking is the last piece of the Invitation Model—and it should be. If you speak before seeking understanding, building trust, and showing how it's done, you may be shouting into a void or blathering uninformed nonsense. By doing the groundwork, you are much more likely to be heard.

Speaking also means advocacy. John Daly, a professor of communication at the University of Texas, Austin, defines advocacy in his book *Advocacy: Championing Ideas and Influencing Others* as "speaking and writing in compelling ways that make decision makers want to adopt your ideas." Whether it is a novel idea, a cause you believe in, or a project you care about, if you need outside support to bring it to life, you cannot do it without advocacy.

Mike Lydon, an urban planner in Miami, had become frustrated with his work. He really cared about making Miami bicycle-friendly, but he wasn't optimistic about the chances. The urban planning process typically involved a lot of discussion, and implementation took a long time. So instead he submitted an opinion piece to the local newspaper proposing a radical idea. What if, for just one day, the city closed a portion of its roads to motor vehicles and only allowed pedestrians and bicyclists?

His op-ed led to a collaboration with other bicycle advocacy groups and an event based on his proposal: Bike Miami Days. No one was more surprised by the results than Lydon, who observes in his book *Tactical Urbanism,* "Big things can happen when you start small." Lydon spoke up about what he cared about, and he set a change in motion.

NO, NO, NO, YES.

Write an Internal Op-Ed

An op-ed, which stands for "opposite the editorial page," is a piece of opinion writing from a guest author that appears in a newspaper or magazine.

Consider what your own op-ed might be. It doesn't have to be a letter to a newspaper (and you don't have to submit it). It can be a thoughtful email that you share with your workmates, a handout for a Friday evening discussion, a call for action in your community, or a blog post about something you feel deserves more attention.

Even if it doesn't get published, writing an op-ed clarifies what you stand for, shows what that might mean, and helps you take a stand or spark a conversation.

You can use the ideas in this chapter to craft the content of your op-ed. First, reflect on what you value and why it matters. Then use the Invitation Model. What is important to the group or organization you are addressing? Why should they care about what you stand for (seek)? Propose ways to try things out or learnings from your own experiments (show). And, of course, write and share the op-ed (speak).

STRONG OPINIONS, DEEPLY FELT

ALRIGHT FOLKS, LET'S TELL PEOPLE WHAT MATTERS! SPEAK TO THEM! CHALLENGE THEM! WHAT DO WE WRITE ABOUT?

WE SHOULD TALK ABOUT WHO WOULD WIN IN A CARBON FOOTPRINT FIGHT BETWEEN ALMOND AND HAZELNUT MILKS.

AH, BUT IT SHOULD BE SOMETHING WITH A WORTHY PURPOSE...

"HOW SPORKS CAN CHANGE THE WORLD!" HOW'S THAT FOR AN OP-ED?

I COULD PUT FORTH A VERY STRONG DEFENSE FOR PINEAPPLE ON PIZZA.

WOOF!

HOW ABOUT THE UNBEARABLE FUTILITY OF EVER SAYING ANYTHING?

Listen to Your Gut

There is one scenario where the "lots of little acts" approach of the Invitation Model may not work: when it comes to standing up for your moral or ethical values in the moment. That's when you need to listen to your gut.

Gut feelings get a bad rap. We have a strong social and cultural imperative to be rational and reasonable and not dwell too much on gut feelings. In fact, they are often equated to subjective opinions. One of my coworkers used to love saying, "My data disagrees with your gut feelings."

Instead of thinking of your gut as being correct or incorrect, think of it as a signaling system. When it signals, it's a good idea to wonder where it is pointing and why.

One of the foremost defenders of our gut feelings is Gerd Gigerenzer, a psychologist who has studied at length how we make decisions and deal with uncertainty. In his book *Gut Feelings: Short Cuts to Better Decision Making,* he defines a gut feeling, a hunch, or intuition as "a judgment that appears quickly in consciousness, whose underlying reasons we are not fully aware of and is strong enough to act upon." According to Gigerenzer, gut feelings are not mere opinions; they are based on unconscious rules that we have learned from experience. Gigerenzer believes this also applies to moral judgments. He writes that just "as a native speaker can tell an incorrect sentence from a correct one without being able to explain why, our set of rules underlying our 'moral grammar' is typically not in awareness." When one of our moral or ethical values is in conflict with a decision, our gut speaks up, and so should you.

On an episode of the podcast *Without Fail,* Andrew Mason, the founder of Groupon, told this story. Groupon had built its business sending customers a once-daily deal—a single email. To grow the business, Mason's team increased to two emails a day. In the short term, the data showed that, while more people than usual unsubscribed from Groupon's mailing list, the increase in purchases made up for that loss. So then they moved on to the next feature, the next experiment, and so on. After a while, the negative

MEET YOUR GUT INSTINCT

THE PHYSICAL GUT
GASTROENTEROLOGIST AND WRITER GIULIA ENDERS NOTES THAT OUR GUT'S NETWORK OF NERVES IS AS LARGE AND CHEMICALLY COMPLEX AS OUR BRAIN'S GRAY MATTER.

THE RIGHT BRAIN
DRAWING EDUCATOR BETTY EDWARDS SAYS WE HAVE TWO WAYS OF KNOWING. THE L-MODE (LEFT BRAIN, COLLOQUIALLY) IS VERBAL, LOGICAL, AND LINEAR; THE R-MODE (RIGHT BRAIN) IS NON-VERBAL, INTUITIVE, AND HOLISTIC.

THE SOUL
MATT KHAN, ONE OF THE MOST-LOVED ART EDUCATORS AT STANFORD, CONSIDERED "FANTASY" AND "SOUL" AS CORE TO DESIGN WORK.

THE HEART
COURAGE COMES FROM THE WORD COR, WHICH MEANS "HEART" IN LATIN.

effects of many such decisions started to catch up with the business. The growth of Groupon's customer base slowed way down, and the company's valuation went with it. Looking back, Mason says that, at the time, the decision didn't feel right, but, like of many us, he left the answer to the data because that felt more rational and objective. Mason's takeaway from that experience was to be clear about when to make decisions based on values and when to make them based on data.

I am not suggesting that you avoid data- and evidence-based decision-making as a tool. Just remember that these are not the only tools. Some decisions have to be based on your values and principles. When your gut sounds the alarm, take a moment to see what it is saying—and find the courage to speak up.

Take a Timeout

There's a thought experiment called the trolley problem that ethicists like to use. It goes like this: A trolley is speeding down a set of railway tracks, about to hit five people tied to the tracks. You are standing next to a lever that will switch the trolley to another track, saving the five people. But on the other track, there is one person tied to the track. What do you do?

Values-based debates often devolve into these kinds of conundrums, where you are forced to choose a lesser evil. But real life is not like the trolley problem, though we often act as if it is. We assume a sense of urgency and think that we have to decide *now,* or that we have limited options. In reality, you can always take more time to figure out a new (and ethical) way.

Watch for situations when your gut signals urgently, telling you that all options are bad (Gerd Gigerenzer calls this feeling "I don't know why, but I know it's wrong"), and ask for a timeout.

Stop. Acknowledge your gut reaction and accept that you don't have a good defense for it, yet. I call this "disagreeing in the moment."

Ask for a timeout. You don't have to have an immediate defense to request time to step back. How much time should you ask for? It depends on your situation. It could be an hour, a week, or even longer.

Use the time you've bought. Figure out what your gut is telling you, seek out what others think, and work together to come up with an alternative solution to resolve the dilemma.

WHO LET THE GUTS OUT?

Values: Conclusion

Values is the second stop on your courage journey. Your beliefs, values, and purpose provide a compass to help you navigate tough dilemmas at home and at work. They give you the spine to stand up for what matters in the world. Although fear the shapeshifter makes its usual appearance, this time in the guise of a precarious wave, your purpose and values help you ride the wave with courage when it really matters.

You've dealt with your fear and reflected on your values. But here's the thing: your fear isn't going to go away, and your purpose may still be a bit fuzzy. It is in this realm of uncertainty that you have to make your choice. What are you going to do? Next up is action—the third stop on your journey.

But first, a little pit stop . . .

WHERE IS THE LINE?

Detour

Good Courage, Bad Courage

How do you know you're on the right side of courage?

When faced with an ethical dilemma, your gut might signal that you are crossing a line. But someone else might see it differently. How can this be true?

Perspective is everything.

The "right thing" can be different for different people. What you value and find purposeful can sometimes be at odds with what others value and find purposeful. Many changemakers look no different from troublemakers at first. Your genuine and honest feedback might make you seem like a jerk to the person receiving it. And yet it might have been the right thing to do.

This is perhaps why William Ian Miller, author of *The Mystery of Courage*, says, "Courage is promiscuous. We are obliged to grant it to nefarious actors and noble ones, to scourges of humanity and benefactors, to enemies and friends."

If perspective is relative, is there any way to be sure that when you act with courage, you are doing the right thing? Nope. As writer and ethicist Rushworth M. Kidder

continued »

Detour, continued

observed, the really tough dilemmas are not right versus wrong, but rather right versus right—situations in which both choices might be right from different perspectives.

You have to act in spite of this ambiguity. In acting with courage, you risk being perceived poorly. You might also just be wrong. That is part of the risk of choosing courage.

There is one scenario that is definitely not courageous: when you bear no risk but others do. A friend stands to lose something by telling you the honest truth about what you need to hear, whereas an internet troll risks nothing. So ask yourself: What are you putting on the line? Risking others purely for your own benefit is not courageous. To be courageous, you yourself must bear the potential consequences of your actions.

So, in the moment, act with integrity based on your purpose and values. Courage calls for us to take action when we don't know how things will play out. Mistakes are inevitable. After all, it is only when you expose your values to the light of the day that you can see whether they need to be reexamined.

If you recognize that your beliefs are misplaced or that you haven't taken responsibility, show courage again. Take time to course-correct, ask for forgiveness, and make things right.

GOOD AND BAD COURAGE

IT'S UP TO YOU

4

in Action

The actual moment of courage feels a lot like taking the stage to perform or speak—while the preparation is scary, the most frightening bit is when the curtain finally goes up and you stand before a live audience.

I am part of a community theater group in Delhi that produces a few plays each year. I'm very familiar with the process of putting together a show and the nervousness, anxiety, and fear that goes with it. First, there is the (gulp) audition. Then, if you survive that and are cast, you have to sweat your way through memorizing your lines. But your fear inevitably hits its apex on the day of the actual performance. Your stomach churns. Your palms sweat. You wonder if you'll make a fool of yourself. You might even eye the backstage door and plot your escape.

THANKFULLY YOU DON'T FLEE... APPLAUSE!

No matter how prepared you are or how hard you've worked to build your capacity for courage—by such practices as taking tiny risks, mitigating the risks ahead, being reflective, and clarifying your purpose and values—at a certain point you can't make things any less scary.

As we have learned, courage is a *when*—and the moment of truth is when you act. If you keep putting it off, and spend your time thinking, planning, and learning instead, the moment will pass you by. The curtain will rise on an empty stage.

I'm using the word *action* broadly here. It is whatever choice, decision, or step you must make. Or not. (Sometimes the courageous choice might be to do nothing.) But even when you don't act, it has to be a deliberate choice.

Overcome the Three Flavors of Inaction

Unfortunately, most of the time when you're not acting it's *not* because you are engaging in courageous civil disobedience. It's because you are stuck, stymied, and spinning our wheels. The first step to getting past this roadside breakdown is to open up the hood and figure out where the problem is. Every courageous action must first get past the inertia of inaction.

Inaction comes in several flavors. One is clear-cut and obvious; the other two are show-stopping charlatans.

Inaction

Inaction is garden-variety avoidance, an all-out shutdown. It's the New Year's resolution without the trip to the gym. It's setting out to write a screenplay, then binge-watching movies instead. (We know this as *procrastination*.) Or it could be a moment in the past, a time when you wish you had acted but didn't. Even so, this flavor of inaction is clear: you know you are avoiding work that needs to be done.

Fauxaction

Fauxaction is fake action. A good example is putting empty platitudes on a company's wall extolling the supposed values of an organization when they aren't reflected in the actual decision-making and behavior. It's like changing your logo when what you really need is a new business plan.

Action

Spinaction

Spinaction is when you're doing a lot, but making zero progress. The word *spin* denotes two ideas: first, that you are just spinning your wheels; and second, that you're putting a positive spin on your predicament—telling yourself that although you're not getting anywhere, you're doing all you can, and there is nothing more you can do. Spinaction is a form of denial. Imagine you have to give critical feedback to someone you care about. You don't want to seem too harsh, so you never really lay it out clearly, hoping they'll still get the message. They don't, but hey, you tried.

Whenever you find yourself stalled, spinning, or faking it, you are avoiding the risks that come with taking *real* action. To recognize these roadblocks and move past them to a stance of action, listen to the reasons for your inaction that you tell yourself. Are they legitimate? Bernard Roth, the d.school's academic director, takes an extreme approach to examining reasons. According to him, "reasons are just excuses prettied up."

Now is the time to use your reflective practice to examine not just your purpose, but also the reasons you are not fulfilling it. If you really care about the purpose, it can help you find the courage to stop making excuses and do what you need to do.

THE FLAVORS OF INACTION

The And/But Switch

Think about a scenario in which you are avoiding taking action. What's your reason? We often use the conjunction "but" to specify our reasons: "I really wish [insert your goal or purpose], but [insert a good reason you can't/aren't accomplishing that]." A good way to examine the legitimacy of your reasons, according to Bernard Roth, is to replace "but" with "and." You'll find that the word "but" is often a way to block yourself. By removing the "but" and replacing it with "and," you switch your stance from closed—there is nothing you can do—to open—something can be done. Now, "your brain has to consider how to deal with both parts of the sentence," Roth says.

Pick a situation in which you are stuck.

Articulate what really matters to you. (Use the reflection tools on page 45.) These are your values and purpose.

State the reasons why you are stuck. I really wish [what you want to do], but [reason why you can't].

Replace the "but" with "and." Notice your internal reaction. Does it force you to revisit the situation with an open mind?

Generate five ideas for how you might proceed.

KICK THE BUT

TWO DEEP BREATHS AND A FEW (DECAF) COFFEES LATER

Face the Moment of Action

You're there. Right before the leap. The moment of action is always ripe with fear—no matter how well you've prepared, you cannot get rid of the risk entirely.

In a letter to his shareholders, Jeff Bezos describes two kinds of decisions:

> **Type 1, or one-way doors:** when you walk through, there is no way back. The decision is irreversible or nearly irreversible.

> **Type 2, or two-way doors:** if you walk through and don't like what you see on the other side, you can always turn around and walk back.

The moment of action always feels like walking through a one-way door (even if it isn't so) . . . the point of no return. It's one thing to earnestly rehearse a conversation about how your relationship isn't working, but saying it to your partner in person is another matter altogether. It's one thing to draw out a plan for quitting your job to start your artisanal bakery, but another to actually follow through. It's one thing to criticize your city council member, but another to run for the seat yourself.

What does this moment of action feel like? Maybe it is a flush of blood to your cheeks. Or a pounding in your heart. Or tension in your shoulders. You may have gotten a little taste of it when you took tiny risks (see page 28), but now you have to eat the whole enchilada.

While researching this book, I asked several people how they muster up courage in the moments they need it most. A number of people invoke a phrase or perform a physical gesture. For example, a CEO I spoke to asks herself, "What would a courageous person do?" A river guide shouts "I am energized, not paralyzed, by fear!" One entrepreneur makes a fist to feel stronger. And an actor told me he puts on an imaginary coat. In the moment of action, a handy tool like a phrase or gesture is a perfect way to steady yourself and set your intention.

Another good phrase comes from Patrick Lencioni, a management theorist and the author of *The Five Dysfunctions of a Team,* a fable about a team that finally comes together. He refers to the moment of action as "entering the danger." Each time a character in his story has to confront a colleague, admit in a social setting that they failed to do their job, or even be the first to speak, they "enter the danger." The danger is the uncomfortable unknown on the other side of these interactions.

Alison Wood Brooks, an experimental psychologist at Harvard, has demonstrated this with her research. There is a fine boundary between the negative emotion of anxiety and the positive emotion of excitement. When people feel a negative emotion (the technical phrase is "negative affective state"), they adopt a threat mindset, whereas a positive emotion switches it to an opportunity mindset. Even a simple statement like "get excited!" can provide that subtle switch. Of course, this does not reduce the actual risks inherent in the situation; it just stops you from focusing on the adverse outcomes. Fear is misdirected energy, and this approach can redirect that energy in a better direction.

FLIP THE FEELING

Design a Mantra or Slogan

Designing a "phrase" is something copywriters often do to foment consumer demand through a product and marketing tagline. You can use that same tactic to power your act of courage. Think of it like a mantra or slogan.

Invoking a mantra might sound hokey, but it's more powerful than you think. *Slogan* is the Gaelic word for "battle cry," and *mantra* is a Sanskrit word with psychological and spiritual powers meant to help the speaker conjure their will. Whatever phrase you choose as a mantra, remember to:

Make it usable. Associate your mantra with a cue. Your cue can be the physical sensation of fear, or an environmental cue, like entering a room. When I voice a counterpoint or a wild idea in a discussion, I like to remind myself to "get through the grimace." People often reflexively grimace when they don't like an idea. That's my cue to call on my mantra, say what I mean without toning it down, and then seek direct reactions afterward.

Make it memorable. Alliteration ("get through the grimace"), rhyming ("energized, not paralyzed"), or powerful language ("enter the danger") makes your mantra easy to recall.

Make more than one. Make different mantras for different scenarios, like starting a new project, owning up to a mistake, or rappelling down a rock face. Use the specificity of a scenario to target one of the faces your fear tries to take on.

Talk and Listen with Courage

How might you practice acting with courage more routinely? Uncomfortable conversations can be a ripe training ground. Giving tough feedback. Addressing a touchy subject. Critiquing someone's work. Saying no to a client request. Setting expectations at your workplace (so you don't have to do yogic contortions to honor every ask). Bringing up an annoying habit with your housemate or spouse. Breakups. These are uncomfortable moments you will visit along the journey of your professional and personal relationships. And they are prime candidates for chickening out. We avoid them (inaction), pretend we're working on them (fauxaction), or work our way around them (spinaction).

At work, you get set up with someone new on a project. You schedule a meeting and they show up late. You give them a wry smile, hoping they will pick up on your annoyance, and get on with the meeting. And then it happens again, and the conversation starts in your head. Should you have said something before? Should you say something now? Or, instead of saying what you really want to say, you wrap up your message to blunt the impact. Consider the classic feedback sh*t sandwich in which critical feedback (the meat) is layered between two thin slices of praise (the bread). If the praise were genuine, the approach could work, but often the praise is empty, there only to cover up what you really want to say.

A LEAK OF THE FEELING

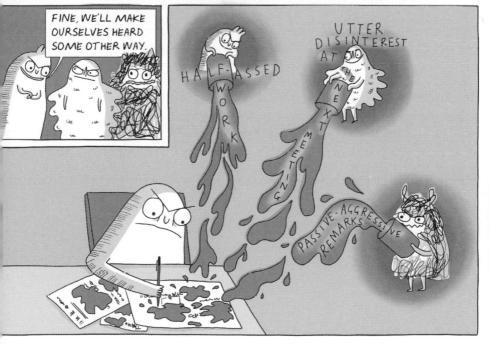

Once again, fear the shapeshifter is doing its handiwork. You avoid these conversations because you fear being disliked (you don't want to seem like a jerk), you fear the consequences (you don't want to make things worse), or, in a clever twist, you fear for the other person (you don't want to hurt anyone's feelings, when you are actually concerned with your own). It's no wonder you choose to stall! In the end, you cannot hide. When you don't express your feelings directly, they get expressed indirectly instead through offhand comments, underhanded gestures, or unapproved changes. Or later, once feelings have festered, they might get expressed as one big explosion, when you finally say "Enough is enough!"

One of the most popular courses at Stanford's Graduate School of Business is called Interpersonal Dynamics, more commonly known as "Touchy Feely." In this class students practice uncomfortable group conversations to learn how their behavior and actions affect others and vice versa. One student framed his biggest takeaway from the course like this: "The feelings we don't express leak out. If you don't express it, you lose the ability to control *how* you express it."

Since you can't stop your feelings from leaking out, the fears that initially kept you from having the conversation will come true. You will seem like a jerk, others will feel hurt, and things will get worse—just very, very slowly and in ways you cannot steer.

So, uncomfortable as it is, you've got to Have. The. Conversation.

Is there a way to have uncomfortable conversations that doesn't feel so . . . uncomfortable? There isn't. Conversations are messy, and there is no One True Way™ to have them. How they unfold will vary based on the situation, the people involved, and even the cultural context. And starting the conversation is just the beginning. Even if you're prepared, you won't know how any particular conversation is going to play out until you are in it.

Navigating a messy conversation is going to be messy, but a simple three-step approach can help:

Frame your feelings.

Set your stance.

Figure out a way forward.

Frame Your Feelings

Use a framework to help you scaffold your feelings through tough conversations. For example, at the d.school, students sharing feedback use the framework "I like [what worked], I wish [what could be better], and what if [a suggestion]?" This framing works well because it sets up the feedback as being about the work and the way people work together (not about the people themselves), and makes it clear that it's okay to criticize, but positivity is welcome too.

Another scaffold is the idea of not crossing "the net," a concept that is also used in Stanford's Touchy Feely class. The net is a metaphorical boundary between what you know and what you don't. You know yourself, your behavior, and how you felt. But you don't really know the

TWO SIDES TO EVERY INTERACTION

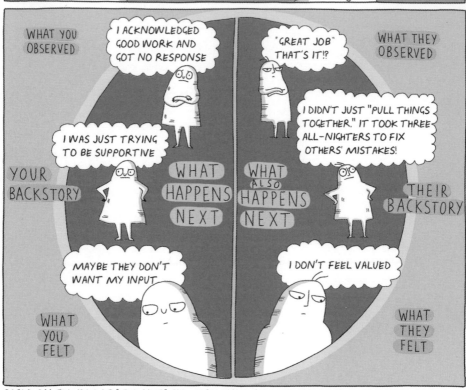

BASED ON THE IDEA OF "THE NET" BY MARY ANN HUCKABAY AND DAVID L. BRADFORD FROM THE STANFORD GRADUATE SCHOOL OF BUSINESS

intentions and motives of the person to whom you are giving feedback. So you frame your feelings like so: "When you do [their behavior or action], I feel [how you felt or thought]." This works in several ways. It acknowledges your feelings, accepts that you don't know the whole story, and invites the other person to share their perspective. Your goal should not be to get the other person to mend their ways or to show them why you are right and they are wrong. The latter isn't a courageous conversation; it is what a 2009 Bollywood film would call emotional "atyachaar" ("torture").

These frameworks aren't silver bullets; they simply help you articulate clearly to yourself what you are feeling and why before you get into an uncomfortable conversation. You still have to dive into the deep end of the pool, but you can think of these frameworks as the lines on the bottom that help you swim straight, or the goggles that help you see, or the ladder on the side that helps you climb out.

Set Your Stance

Once you've framed your feelings, you have to share them. Having the right stance during the conversation can make all the difference.

In this case, your stance does not mean your opinion. It is more like a stance you would take in sports—a deliberate posture of preparedness. You're not being defensive, blocking like a linebacker; you're instead ready to pivot, shoot, pass, or move quickly like a basketball player. (Yes, I've used four sports metaphors in as many pages. I promise, that's it.) The two key features of this stance—the legs you're standing on—are clarity and openness.

Clarity is saying what you actually think and feel. Be careful not to say what you *think* you should feel or *imagine* you should say, and don't try to control what the other person feels. Openness is leaving room in the conversation for you to be wrong. Accept that this conversation serves your relationship (not just you), and strive to learn about others' points of view.

As a manager, I have often avoided the uncomfortable conversation in which I must let a prospective candidate know that they did not get the job. At the end of an interview, they would ask when they would hear from me, and I would say, "We'll get back to you," even when I already knew they would not be hired. I didn't want them to feel rejected. So I didn't tell them anything. I had perfected the art of professional ghosting.

I confided to Scott Doorley, the d.school's creative director, that I found it hard to be direct, because I wanted to be kind. To me, directness is synonymous with being rude. Doorley countered by saying, "That's a false dichotomy. You can be direct and kind." His response gave me pause.

The next time a candidate came in, and I realized that we didn't have a role that fit their work experience, I changed my stance. When the candidate asked, "When will I hear from you?" I reminded myself that I can be direct and kind (a mantra!). I told her that we couldn't hire her and explained why. Instead of being disheartened, she thanked me for not leaving her hanging, and added, "Most companies

THE LET'S-GET-THIS-TOUGH-CONVO-GOING-STANCE

ALRIGHT BUDDY, YOU'RE HAVING THIS TOUGH CONVO. BE CLEAR AND OPEN.

YOU BET, I'M GOING TO BE CLEAR AS DAY, GRR.

CAN I FIX YOUR STANCE? KEEP YOUR BACK STRAIGHT. THEY CALL IT "HAVING A SPINE" FOR A REASON.

I'M VERTICAL. ISN'T THAT STANCE-Y ENOUGH?

ARMS OPEN, PALMS VISIBLE!

FOLDED ARMS MEANS YOU ARE BEING DEFENSIVE. I LEARNED THIS FROM IMPROV THEATER!

HEY! I WAS COLD.

GOOD THING WE ARE WARMING UP.

AND LET'S GET THAT FROWN OFF!

FLICK!   *WHEE!*   *PING!*

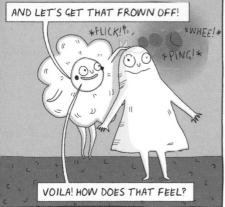

VOILA! HOW DOES THAT FEEL?

A BIT LIKE I'M IN A MUSICAL AND ABOUT TO BURST INTO SONG, BUT ... OKAY?

YEP, AND IT WORKS! NOW GO GET 'EM!

leave candidates in limbo and I have to keep following up."
(Gulp.) Often speed and clarity are kindness enough.

Your stance, or how you show up for a challenging conversation, can mean as much as what you say.

Figure Out a Way Forward

What happens next? You won't know until you have the conversation. Once you and others have had time to process and synthesize what you learned and how you felt, you figure out a way forward. Because a way forward really should be your goal. It is not about focusing the attention on ourselves, or even on our team members; what really deserves attention is the space between the people.

I call this strange space between me and my collaborators the Collab-a-blob. Taking on the shape and texture of your collaboration, the Collab-a-blob matures as you build trust, navigate conflict, and cocreate things. It's what your collaboration looks like at any given moment. Just like any other creature (even if metaphorical), the Collab-a-blob needs to eat. Courageous, free-range communication and feedback are its sustenance, and a lack of this food makes the Collab-a-blob weak and spiky. Although the chefs may encounter short-term emotional discomfort as they debate ingredients and methods, when the Collab-a-blob is nurtured with good communication, it becomes big and robust and delightfully blobulous.

If you examine your relationships in work and life, you will notice that you work well with some people and are still figuring out how to do so with others. The same is true for them. Good relationships aren't just about the people involved; they are the sum of how those people relate to one another when they are together. Every team's Collab-a-blob is a little bit different.

Paying attention to the contours of the space between people can help you recognize the singular nature of each team or partnership. When you engage in a difficult conversation, you expose these contours, acknowledge and accept one another's constraints, and either create new norms and rules (see page 34) or, when it makes sense, agree to part ways.

Having difficult conversations is perhaps one of the most frequent acts of everyday courage you will get a chance to undertake. Courage is a habit, and having these conversations is a great way to build that habit.

BEHOLD, THE COLLAB-A-BLOB

Have. The. Conversation!

Think of a professional or personal relationship in which you've been holding something back; your feelings are starting to leak and affect the way you work together. It sounds like an uncomfortable conversation is in order. Here's a (comic) cheat sheet to help you get through it.

Action: Conclusion

The moment of action, the third stop on your courage journey, really does feel like a leap. A one-way door. A point of no return. This moment is the *when* of courage. Even after you have tangled with your fear and made friends with your values and purpose, you don't have a black or white answer. There is no green light telling you to go or red light telling you to stop. It is an unmarked road to an uncertain destination, and you have to decide whether or not to hit the gas pedal.

It is also the transition point between the world as it was before and the world as it is going to be. Well, what the heck does that mean?

Onward to the final stop of your courage journey: change.

THERE WILL BE CONSEQUENCES

5

Change

Your journey is well under way. You've picked up some tools, and you're ready to act with courage.

But what happens after you do? It might go well: Things work out. You find that your fears were unfounded. You resolve a conflict. You feel great about upholding your values. You inspire others by acting courageously—your story gives them permission to try something new in their own life. Hooray!

Or it might not go so well: You speak up but are silenced. Your bravery is met with ridicule. Or worse, you get fired. Your choice to be clear and open is met with anger and pushback. You lose time and money. You fail. You trusted your gut, but it led you down the wrong path. Boooo!

Or it may not be so clear: You're stuck in limbo—you can't tell whether things are going well or badly, and you're not sure if you should keep going or just quit. You made a little progress, but maybe not enough. Hmmm . . .

No matter which category your act falls into, one thing is certain: things changed. Real consequences, both positive and negative, give acts of courage gravity. They are the source of our fears and an expression of our values. But consequences are not resolutions. Our journey keeps going. Pema Chödrön, a Buddhist teacher, wrote in her book *When Things Fall Apart,* "Things don't really get solved. They come together and they fall apart. Then they come together again and fall apart again. It's just like that." Exploring the consequences of your actions helps create a road map for the way forward.

NOW WHAT !?

WHEN THINGS WORKED OUT

WHEN THINGS DIDN'T WORK OUT

WHEN THERE IS MORE TO COME

This last leg of the courage journey is more like a perpetual refueling and retooling station than an end point. Here you face the following questions: What came together? What fell apart? What did you learn? And, of course, what happens next?

Reframe to Recourage

The bad news first: failure, mistakes, and missteps are all inevitable parts of the courage journey.

Maybe you bombed on stage. Or got rejected from a college you worked hard to get into. Or fell out of love. The specifics of your failure depend on your story and what you call a failure. In hindsight, the bold or courageous act can feel stupid and reckless. Your fear gets to scream, "I told you so!" It feels like a gut punch when what you set out to do doesn't work out.

You certainly know the phrase "Once bitten, twice shy." The Hindi variant is more colorful: "Doodh ka jala chaach bhi phoonk phoonk ke peeta hai." It means: "If your tongue has been burned, you will even blow on (cold) buttermilk to cool it." All failures have a buttermilk phase. After all, failure is an encounter with the real world—and in the real world, you can get burned. The future seems bleak, and your defenses are up even when they don't need to be. Failure doesn't just cost time, money, or reputation; It can also leave you feeling discouraged.

The length and intensity of your buttermilk phase depends on the severity of the failure, the type of risk you took, and how you feel about it. It's okay to want to cool the butter-milk. But don't wallow in the buttermilk phase indefinitely. Even Banksy, the famous graffiti artist, has had buttermilk phases. He is known to have said, "If you are tired, learn to rest, not quit." Sometimes it takes a bit of courage just to rest. When you find yourself blowing on the buttermilk one time too many, it's time for a reframe to help you recourage.

Michael Barry and Sara Beckman, designers and educa-tors at Stanford and the University of California, Berkeley, often pose this question to their students: How would you build a bridge? The students ask for details like the dis-tance the bridge needs to cover, the type of bridge it needs to be, and so on. Then the students are asked to get people

to the other side of a river. With the problem restated, the solutions change: a boat, a tunnel, a zipline.

This classic design technique is *reframing*—looking at a problem in a new way to reveal new possibilities. Reframing in real life can be a bit tricky because it requires you to revisit your assumptions and biases. Still, the idea is simple: when you change your perspective, you change your perception: both what you notice and how you think about it.

The tale you tell yourself after experiencing a big or small failure is the frame you have chosen for that failure. I call these "bad-time stories." To escape your buttermilk phase, you have to reframe these stories. For example: Let's say Sam and Kathy each open a lemonade stand. Both have a not-so-great first day. After sitting in the sun for the entire afternoon, neither has sold a single glass. Sam's frame for this tiny failure is "I can't even sell lemonade. It's probably going to be like this for the rest of the season; I better cut my losses." Kathy's frame, on the other hand, is "Today was a bummer. Maybe people weren't that thirsty."

We each have our own take. University of Pennsylvania psychologist Martin Seligman calls these differences in framing "explanatory styles." I find these two dimensions particularly useful:

Permanence: Explaining things in a permanent way (It's going to be like this for the rest of the season) versus a temporary way (Today was a bad one).

Personalization: Explaining things based on internal reasons (I can't even sell lemonade) versus external reasons (People weren't thirsty).

TIME FOR A REFRAME

THE FLEXI-FIT

FOR AN ADAPTABLE VIEW

CORITA KENT'S FINDER

FOR SEEING THE WHOLE, ONE LITTLE PIECE AT A TIME

EXTRA-WIDE PANORAMIC

FOR A BIGGER VIEW

THE "HANDMADE"

FOR A PERSONAL ASPECT

THE LATERAL

FOR AN UNSEEN PERSPECTIVE

THE "FANCY"

WITH ADDED SILVER LINING, FOR AN OPTIMISTIC OUTLOOK

How does this apply to recouraging? When you frame your failures as unchangeable (permanent) and feel that *you* are the reason you failed (internal), you are more likely to be discouraged. Such a bad-time story, which Seligman calls a "pessimistic explanatory style," keeps you in the buttermilk phase for longer. Luckily, Seligman and his team also found that you can learn to reframe your failures and change your bad-time stories. They call this capability "learned optimism."

This reframe requires only a couple of steps. The first is to notice the stories you tell yourself when you experience a setback, and how they make you feel. The second is to challenge yourself to dispute your standard narrative and switch your explanations from permanent (*It will always be this way*) to temporary (*It happened only this one time and things can change*), and from entirely internal (*I suck at this*) to somewhat external (*Maybe it's not just me, and there are some things I can't control*).

There is nuance here: courage is about taking responsibility. This is not a story to tell others to deflect blame or thwart personal growth—it is a reframe to tell yourself in order to bounce back. The truth is, whether we succeed or fail, the responsibility is always partly ours and partly circumstance. This trick just helps you focus on both, especially if you tend to only berate yourself.

Reframing can give you the fuel to recover and recourage. (Yes, that's a word now.) Then, you can contend with the real-world consequences of what happened, whatever they may be.

The Four Reframes

Start by noticing your bad-time story. What setback did you encounter? How did you (or more likely, fear the shapeshifter) explain it to yourself? Watch out for permanent versus temporary explanations and internal versus external explanations and notice how they make you feel.

Next, try the four reframes (inspired by Martin Seligman's ABCDE technique):

Reframe 1—aka the Sherlock: Are you focusing too much on one particular setback, and ignoring other times you have succeeded? Grab your hunting cap and magnifying glass and search for missing evidence.

Reframe 2—aka the Bricolage: *Bricolage* is something created from a wide range of materials. What are all the other reasons that may have caused the setback, especially those that were out of your control?

Reframe 3—aka the Choose Your Adventure: Sure, this bad-time story may be (somewhat) accurate, but what you do next is up to you. Change how the story unfolds, pick a new path.

Reframe 4—aka the Talk to the Hand!: Dismiss it! Yes, you may be at fault, and this may be a pattern; that is, the story is true. But is it useful holding on to it? If it stops you from recouraging, don't.

When Things Work Out

Plow pose is an inverted asana in yoga in which you lie down on your back and swing your legs up and over your head until your toes touch the floor behind your head. While you feel a stretch in your glutes and hamstrings, this is the kind of pose that makes you aware of muscles you didn't know you had in places you didn't know you had them. Courage is like that too. Once you find yourself acting courageously, you're sure to discover moxie muscles you didn't even know were there.

Courage is about risk. Risk means you don't know how things are going to play out. When you act with courage, you are always in for a surprise. Sometimes that surprise is an unpleasant one, like failure. Other times you step up, act with courage, and not only do things go well, but they go better than expected.

I've seen this often, both as a student and as an educator at the d.school, where students are pushed to take a creative risk. George Kembel, one of the d.school's cofounders, used to say that the d.school is about creating innovators, not innovations. At what moment do students think of themselves as innovators? It's when they surprise themselves. Over and over again, I've heard students say, "I never thought I could do that," or "I didn't think I could come up with something from scratch." They discover muscles they never knew existed. That is the gift of courage. Whether you discover it through a moment or through many acts of everyday courage, courage can help you see your own agency in bringing change. And that is what you take into the world, what sets the stage for big changes to come.

Look at Ben Knelman. Ben studied Russian literature and economics as an undergraduate at Stanford, and he expected to work as an economist with the government or the United Nations. He told me that even as an all-star Stanford undergraduate, he was petrified about taking even an introductory workshop at the d.school. Instead of using his expertise in his area of study, he would have to interview the person sitting next to him in class, understand their backstory, and design something for them. This prospect was so scary to Ben that he decided he wouldn't apply.

But then he chose to move toward fear, not away from it. It was this choice that later pushed him to take a full quarter d.school class. During his student project, he spoke to a few janitors who worked the night shift at Stanford, and he learned that they wanted to save money but couldn't seem to. He created a simple messaging-based system to remind the janitors to save, and it helped. Ben's system eventually became a microfinance company called Juntos, which now has now served millions of people. That's how everyday courage adds up. What begins with an awkward moment can become an impactful contribution to the world. Juntos started in 2010 and was acquired in 2021 by Nubank, a Latin American financial services company. Ben and his team now serve many more people around the world. He is still doing economics but is using a different medium than he originally expected. He traces his success back to the courage muscles he discovered in the process of taking a risk.

TAKES ONE TO GROW ONE

When Things Are Unclear

A definitive win is cause for celebration, and a definitive failure is cause for some despair, but at least you know whether things went one way or another. Sometimes the most excruciating outcome is when you tried . . . and then you have no idea whether it was worth it! You volunteered to start a sustainability initiative at your organization, got assurances that your organization will take it up next quarter, and then . . . nothing. You started a business, found a customer or a few, but now everything seems to be plateauing. Are you on the right track? You can't quite tell. In this case, what is your next move? Should you quit, or should you keep going? And if you do keep going, how much longer might you have to go?

There are advocates on both sides. Economists talk about the sunk cost fallacy that applies when you keep pursuing something because you have put too much material (or emotional) resources into it and are trying to recover those sunk costs. Their advice: quit. On the flip side, sometimes the right answer is to keep going. This is especially true when the stakes are high and the problem is complicated. Change takes time, and when it takes time, it's hard to see whether it's working while you are doing it.

In an essay on hope in *The Guardian*, the writer and historian Rebecca Solnit recounts civic movements and acts of courage that inspired other activists decades later. She says that the "true impact of activism may not be felt for a

DONUT WORRY

generation. That alone is reason to fight, rather than surrender to despair." That's true for civic impact and personal transformation. Tushar Vashisht, founder of the wellness company HealthifyMe, once told me that it takes one thousand days to see the light in business. That's nearly three years just to see the light; who knows how much longer till daybreak?

In the world of design, an attempt that is meant to be quittable is called a prototype. It is quittable because criteria for when to quit are laid out beforehand—if you test it and it doesn't work, you can discard it. It is also quittable because the resources you put into making and testing a prototype aren't high, so you don't feel attached to it. Prototyping can give you the courage to stay on track or try something new. The idea of a prototype can be applied to both the path and how you navigate it. If your business isn't working (path), you could try a different marketing strategy (how you navigate it), or try a different business (a new path). It depends on how widely you are willing to cast the net of what you call a prototype, and how sure you are of whether it is working.

The answer might also lie with the second stop of the courage journey: your purpose and values. You have to give yourself permission to do what feels right to you based on your values. Sometimes the answer might be to quit. Other times it might be to go on. And either way, somebody will tell you that you chose wrong. Courage is both accepting what you choose and trusting that you can change course later if you need to.

The Change Log

We all have people whose work and life we admire and use as a model—our heroes. Their stories can seem neatly wrapped, but that's never the whole story. To challenge the narrative of easy success, I go looking for the embarrassing beginnings of the people I admire.

I dig through internet archives and look at old websites. Or watch the earliest performance of great comic stars. I'll scroll to the first post or image of a longtime and popular blogger. By creating a Change Log, I get a peek into their evolution. It is akin to looking at photos of your younger self and wincing at your terrible taste in hair and fashion. There is a lot of awkward out there.

This is not an exercise in schadenfreude—the German word for taking pleasure in someone else's misfortune—but rather an exercise in comradeship. Even when they were churning out embarrassing work or failing, they found the courage to keep going.

You can also do this for a social or cultural change that you now take for granted but that took years to happen. Trace the acts of courage that many people had to undertake to get it there.

You can do this with your own work, too. Pick something you've mastered and look back at your early attempts. After you shake your head at the sight of that mullet, thank your past self for persevering.

IT TAKES A FEW TRIES

YEAR 5 — THE PIGTAILS

YEAR 7 — THE HELMET

YEAR 9 — THE WOLVERINE

YEAR 12 — THE MULLET

YEAR 15 — THE UNDERCUT

YEAR 17 — THE PERM OF DREAMS

Change: Conclusion

Congratulations! You've reached the end of the courage journey. Or have you?

You know you haven't. A single act of everyday courage is never an end. The next moment for courage is right around the corner, if not staring you in the face right now.

Change, the last destination of your courage journey, is another journey in itself. It comes with buttermilk phases, bad-time stories, unclear next steps, and surprise wins. And you respond to this change by figuring out what to do next.

Whether your act of courage paid off, went sideways, or produced the all-too-common inconclusive results, I hope it spurs you on to choose courage again, every day.

EPILOGUE: RAISE A GLASS

Epilogue

When, like me, you learn how to drive in a country like India, where traffic rules are a little lax, inevitably you will hit the car ahead of you or get hit by the car behind you. These unavoidable fender-benders are usually followed by a heated argument—for the entertainment of the gathering crowd and for the drivers involved—to establish who was at fault.

I had watched my friends do it, and to my teenage self, this act of bravado seemed like a rite of passage that accompanied learning how to drive. Except I found the whole exercise to be a bit stupid. And when my time came, I was reluctant to engage. The accident had happened. It was done. I wondered why we couldn't just assess the damage and figure out a way forward. Wasn't that the smart thing to do?

Yes, moving on was the wise thing to do. And yet, when I did it, without a dramatic squabble, I felt like a coward. How was I supposed to feel? What was I supposed to do? Are being wise and being brave at odds with each other? It's a question I have thought about for a long time.

Courage is a choice. Courage is when you choose to be brave *and* wise. Courage is when you use your wisdom to know what matters to you and you use your bravery to act in spite of the risks. Too much wisdom and too little bravery and you end up with inaction. Too much bravery and too little wisdom ends in recklessness (and maybe a fight in the middle of the road in Delhi).

So, when is courage?

Courage is when your inner values match your outer actions. Hopefully you do it every day—even if just in small ways. It will all add up, ~~but~~ *and* it's still up to you.

Recommended Reading

The Achievement Habit: Stop Wishing, Start Doing, and Take Command of Your Life by Bernard Roth (New York: Harper Business, 2015)

Bird by Bird: Some Instructions on Writing and Life by Anne Lamott (New York: Pantheon Books, 1994)

Design Thinking: Understanding How Designers Think and Work by Nigel Cross (Oxford, England: Berg Publishers, 2011)

Gut Feelings: The Intelligence of the Unconscious by Gerd Gigerenzer (New York: Viking Adult, 2007)

How Good People Make Tough Choices: Resolving the Dilemmas of Ethical Living by Rushworth M. Kidder (New York: William Morrow, 1995)

Learned Optimism: How to Change Your Mind and Your Life by Martin Seligman (New York: Knopf, 1991)

Shoe Dog: A Memoir by the Creator of Nike by Phil Knight (New York: Scribner, 2016)

Thinking in Systems: A Primer by Donella Meadows (White River Junction, VT: Chelsea Green, 2008)

The War of Art: Break Through the Blocks and Win Your Inner Creative Battles by Steven Pressfield (New York: Rugged Land, 2002)

Why Loiter? Women and Risk on Mumbai Streets by Shilpa Phadke (New Delhi: Penguin Random House India, 2011)

Acknowledgments

Thank you: To the d.school, for being a font of strength and courage for me wherever I am in the world.

To Scott Doorley and Charlotte Burgess-Auburn, for giving me the opportunity to write this book, expertly guiding me through the process, patiently listening to my frustrations, and creating space for me to surprise myself with things I never thought I could do.

To Ruby Elliot, for taking my amateur scribbles and dialogue and transforming them into real comics with both levity and depth.

To Julie Bennett, my editor; Annie Marino, my book designer; Hannah Rahill, Emma Campion, Kelly Booth, Jane Chinn, and all the amazing people at Ten Speed Press. You know how to level things up.

To all the people who shared their stories of courage with me: Gaurav Baheti, Taylor Cone, Hamsa Ganesh, Nishita Gill, Somya Hastekar, Nikhil Jambagi, Ben Knelman, Amarjeet Kumar, Dhruv Lohumi, Aditya Pattanath, Swati Seth, Sneha Virmani, and Molly Clare Wilson.

To my parents, Avinash Goel and Uma Rani: your love and support always get me out of my buttermilk phases. I love you.

To my brothers, Gaurav and Sameer, who see the world in such different ways that it always forces me to reflect on my own worldview.

Finally, to Zomato. Without the opportunity to lead, the room to fail, and the challenges I had to navigate on the job, I might've never noticed my own courage gap.

Index

Copyright © 2022 by The Board of Trustees of the Leland Stanford Junior University on behalf of Hasso Plattner Institute of Design
Illustrations copyright © 2022 by Ruby Elliot

Published in the United States by Ten Speed Press, an imprint of Random House, a division of Penguin Random House LLC, New York.
www.tenspeed.com

Ten Speed Press and the Ten Speed Press colophon are registered trademarks of Penguin Random House LLC.

Library of Congress Cataloging-in-Publication Data
Names: Goel, Ashish, author. | Elliot, Ruby (Author), illustrator.
Title: Drawing on courage: risks worth taking and stands worth making / Ashish Goel.
Description: First edition. | California : Ten Speed Press, [2022] | Illustrations by Ruby Elliot.
Identifiers: LCCN 2020031225 (print) | LCCN 2020031226 (ebook) | ISBN 9781984857989 (trade paperback) | ISBN 9781984857996 (ebook)
Subjects: LCSH: Courage--Comic books, strips, etc. | Creation (Literary,artistic, etc.)--Psychological aspects--Comic books, strips, etc.
Classification: LCC BJ1533.C8 G64 2021 (print) | LCC BJ1533.C8 (ebook) | DDC 179/.6--dc23
LC record available at https://lccn.loc.gov/2020031225
LC ebook record available at https://lccn.loc.gov/2020031226

Paperback ISBN: 978-1-9848-5798-9
eBook ISBN: 978-1-9848-5799-6

Printed in China

Acquiring editor: Hannah Rahill | Editor: Julie Bennett
Designer: Annie Marino | Art director: Emma Campion | Production designer: Mari Gill
Typefaces: Hope Meng's d.sign, The Designers Foundry's Wulkan Display, and Dinamo's Whyte
Production manager: Jane Chinn
Copyeditor: Kristi Hein | Proofreader: Emily K. Wolman | Indexer: Ken DellaPenta
Publicist: David Hawk | Marketers: Daniel Wikey and Windy Dorresteyn
d.school creative team: Scott Doorley, Charlotte Burgess-Auburn, and Nariman (Nadia) Gathers

10 9 8 7 6 5 4 3 2 1

First Edition